FOLD AND CUT STORIES

by Jerry J. Mallett
and Timothy S. Ervin

Alleyside Press

Cover art by Pat Topper

Published by Alleyside Press, a Division of Freline, Inc.
P. O. Box 889
Hagerstown, MD 21741

ISBN 0–913853–26–7

Printed in the United States of America

Contents

About Storytelling 5

Where Does Your Father Work? 7

A Sharp Texas Tall Tale 9

The Great Race 11

The One-Half Story 14

The Thing with Three Humps 17

Will It Ever Snow? 20

My Uncle, the Artist 23

Jacob's Gift 27

Uncle Merlin's Magic 29

Samuel Seagull 32

The Magic Forest 35

Gussy G. 37

Where Is Pepito? 40

The Hiking Incident 44

The Muddywater Mystery 48

The Spoiled Princess 51

About Storytelling

The Value of Storytelling

People the world over have always been fascinated by stories. In earlier centuries, storytelling was a valuable social skill. The storyteller enjoyed considerable prestige and was depended on for entertainment, relaxation, and enlightenment.

Learning the ancient art of storytelling is well worth the effort for the pleasure it affords both the teller *and* the audience. When the librarian or teacher uses storytelling in the library or classroom, the students are directly and intimately involved with the story. Storytelling allows the teller to move around, use gestures and eye contact, clown a bit, and even involve the listeners as characters in the story. These things can make stories come alive for listeners.

Storytelling also helps children become familiar with story language and story structures. Familiarity with these aspects helps them read stories themselves more easily and enjoy them more. It also helps in introducing them to the plots and themes that run through all literature.

In addition, storytelling provides the stimulus for children's storytelling. Seeing the librarian or teacher engage in storytelling helps children understand that storytelling is a worthy activity, and motivates them to tell their own stories.

Choosing the Story

The most important factor in choosing a story is to select one that is really *enjoyable*. The narrator should enjoy spending time preparing the story and retelling it with conviction and enthusiasm. It must also fit the narrator's personality, style, and talents. This is important because whatever pleasure the narrator derives from telling the story is conveyed to the children.

Storytelling demands an appreciative audience. Therefore, the selected story must also be *appropriate* for the listeners. The storyteller must be aware of children's interests, ages, and experience. Young children have short attention spans, so story length must be considered when selecting a tale. Children's ages will also influence the subject matter of the tale. Young children like stories about familiar subjects such as animals, children, or home life. They respond to the repetitive language in cumulative tales and enjoy joining in when appropriate. Children from roughly ages seven through ten enjoy folktales with longer plots. Older children enjoy adventure tales, myths, and legends.

Whatever the choice, the storyteller must *feel at ease* with the material, must *enjoy* the story, and must want to *share* it with others.

Preparing the Story for Telling

Storytelling does not require memorization, but it does require preparation. Certain steps will help the storyteller prepare for this enjoyable experience.

First, divide the story into units of action—that is, identify the major events of the plot. If you strip away the descriptive material, most stories easily divide into definable series of actions.

The second step is to identify any recurring phrases or refrains that need to be memorized. For example, in *Jack and the Beanstalk,* the giant consistently declares, "Fee Fi Fo Fum, I smell the blood of an Englishman." This needs to be told exactly as it appears in the story in order to retain the spirit of the tale.

The third step is to practice telling the story until you feel at ease and are sure you will remember it. It is advisable to use a tape recorder to evaluate your presentation for pitch, enunciation, timing, and expression.

Fold and Cut Stories

This book, *Fold and Cut Stories,* highlights a special storytelling technique, the cutting of a piece of folded paper as the story is told. This popular type of story is unique in that the development of the plot coincides with the folding and cutting of a sheet of paper, so that a cut-out picture, corresponding to the point of the story, is completed as the story ends. Older children try to guess the pictorial conclusion beforehand, with the aid of the clues given within the context of the story and partially completed cut-out. But younger children are often quite surprised when they see the finished product. Either way results in a lot of fun for everyone involved! Good fold and cut stories all have the elements of surprise and suspense and present a challenge for children at any level.

Knowing what the completed cut-out will look like is a tremendous help for remembering the story sequence. The detailed patterns included in this book make the sequence of the story easy to develop and remember. All that is necessary is to be certain to hold the pattern in the right position and follow the dotted line cuts shown in the illustrations. (Suggestion: You might want to draw light pencil cut lines on the paper, which your audience will not be able to see.) The words where the cutting action are appropriate are printed in CAPITAL LETTERS. (Unspoken directions are given in italics and in parentheses.)

A story's sequence of action is revealed in the paper cuts that develop toward the culmination of the story. The finished cut-out makes the point of the story—often in a surprising or humorous way. The use of such a visual aid has the added feature of acting as an attention-holder for the audience.

Where Does Your Father Work?

Preparation

You will need a sheet of 8½ x 11" paper and scissors for this story. Fold the sheet of paper in half, lengthwise, as shown in the illustration.

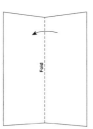

Paper position for story

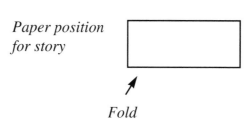

Fold

Be sure to hold the fold *downward* and make your cuts exactly as shown in the illustrations; otherwise the finished product will not work.

Tell the following story while making the cuts as shown in the illustrations.

Grace lives **IN THIS HOUSE** with her family.

Grace has a very normal family with one exception: Her father has a most unusual job. It used to embarrass Grace to tell the other kids what her father did, but now she is very proud.

Grace's father gets up very early in the morning to go to his job. The first thing he does is to **OPEN THE GARAGE DOOR** and back his car out of the garage.

Next, he drives many miles **DOWN A LONG, STRAIGHT HIGHWAY.**

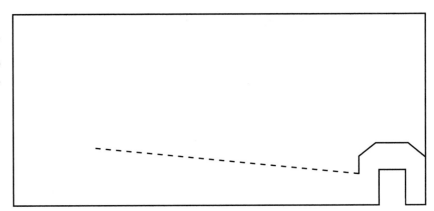

Next, he parks his car and walks out on a **LONG DOCK.**

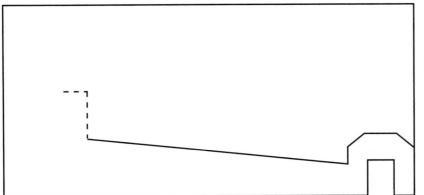

Then, he rides in a small boat **AROUND THE BAY** to get to where he works.

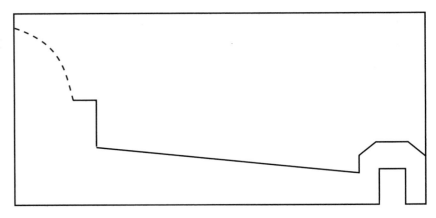

Do you think you can guess where Grace's father works? *(Unfold the paper.)*

A Sharp Texas Tall Tale

Preparation

You will need a sheet of 8½ x 11" paper (preferrably, gold or yellow) and scissors for this story. Fold the sheet of paper in half, lengthwise, as shown in the illustration.

Fold

*Paper position
for story*

Be sure to hold the fold *upwards* and make your cuts exactly as shown in the illustrations; otherwise the finished product will not work.

Tell the following story while making the cuts as shown in the illustrations.

The annual Texas County Fair was just around the corner. Now the Texas County Fair wasn't just any fair. It was Ohio's most unusual fair. You see, Texas County wasn't just another county in Ohio; it was like another state. It was simply like living in the state of Texas. They did things up big in Texas County. The fair, for example has the longest midway of any fair in the United States. **IT STARTED OUT AS A NARROW THING BUT GOT WIDER ALONG ITS 200-MILE PATH.**

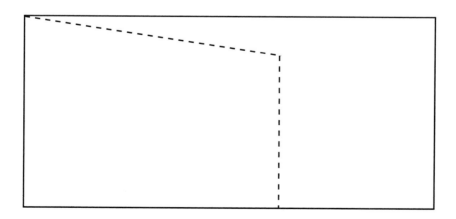

Every year they had a quilting contest at the fair. The winner got a mighty special trophy. So you can understand why everyone wanted his or her quilt to win. Months before the fair you could find everyone **SITTING AROUND THEIR TABLES** quilting until they thought their fingers would fall off.

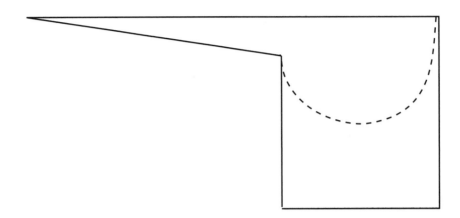

The opening day of the fair finally came. The quilting judging was right after the opening parade. The quilters, however, weren't in a hurry. You see, the parade usually lasted about four days. They really do things in a big way in Texas County!

The first four days passed and the quilting judging began. Old Clara Wilkers was sure she'd win. But when they opened her folded quilt, everyone gasped in horror. A big piece had been eaten **RIGHT OUT OF THE MIDDLE** of Clara's quilt. She was heartbroken.

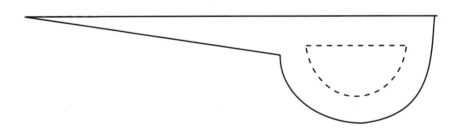

After two weeks, the judging was finally over. It usually took longer, but because the school year was starting, they only looked at the first 3,000 quilts. They really do things big in Texas County!

Tommy and Tina Hantyson were the winners. They had quilted a Texas State Flag. They proudly accepted their trophy—a giant pair of solid gold scissors! *(Unfold the paper.)*

The Great Race

Preparation

You will need a sheet of 8½ x 11" paper and scissors for this story. Fold the sheet of paper in half, lengthwise, as shown in the illustration.

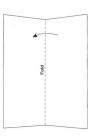

Paper position for story

Fold

Be sure to hold the fold *downward* and make your cuts exactly as shown in the illustrations; otherwise the finished product will not work.

Tell the following story while making the cuts as shown in the illustrations.

It was the day of the great race and all the townsfolk were gathered on **THE SMALL KNOLL** outside of Tiddlewinkville.

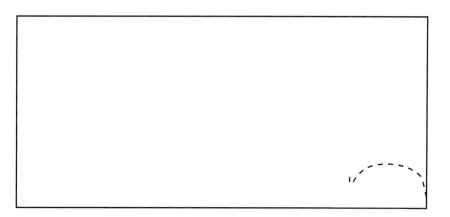

This race was the showdown between Hercules, the big-mouthed bragging rabbit, and Melvin, the quiet, modest turtle. It seems that Hercules had teased Melvin once too often about his slowness. That's when Melvin challenged the rabbit to a race. The townsfolk were there in support of Melvin, even though everyone knew Hercules was bound to win the race. After all, rabbits are by nature much faster than turtles.

Hercules and Melvin were crouched at the starting line as the gun went off, signaling the start of the race. Hercules bounded from the starting line and Melvin hurriedly crept after him.

The first part of the race was **ACROSS THE FIELD AND DOWN THE LANE.**

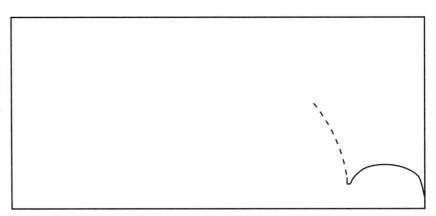

The townsfolk shook their heads as Hercules left Melvin in a trail of dust.

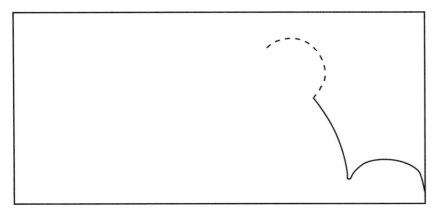

When Hercules reached the river, he turned to see where Melvin was. He laughed when he saw Melvin just beginning to cross the field. He decided not to tire himself out and so he jogged **OVER THE BRIDGE.**

The next part of the race was following Old River Road. Even though Hercules was far in the lead, he decided to continue jogging **DOWN THE ROAD.**

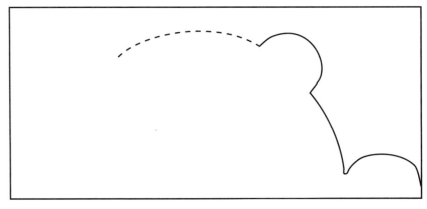

As Hercules reached the last part of the race, McDonald's Woods, he spied **A LARGE, SMOOTH ROCK.**

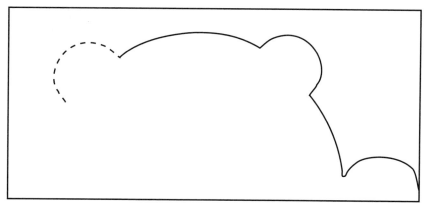

It looked so comfortable and he was so far ahead of Melvin that Hercules decided to take a little rest. Well, he no sooner leaned back on that smooth rock than he went right to sleep.

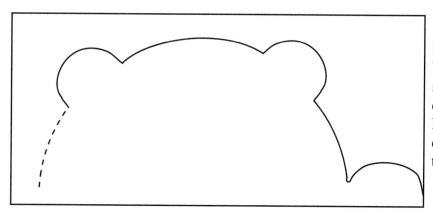

After about an hour, Melvin reached McDonald's Woods. He noticed Hercules sleeping on the rock and very quietly he slipped past him. He hurried, as fast as a turtle can, **DOWN THE PATH** through McDonald's Woods.

After a while, Hercules awoke with a start. He had no idea just how long he had been sleeping, so he immediately took off running at top speed through McDonald's Woods. As he came out of the woods, he heard the crowd yelling and he ran even faster toward the finish line. He saw Melvin nearing the finish line and so he ran even faster.

To this day, the townsfolk still talk about that great race and on whom **THE FINISH LINE FLAG** was dropped.

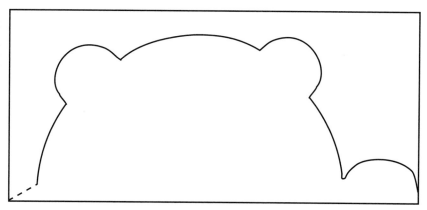

Do you think you know who won the race? *(Unfold the paper.)*

The One-Half Story

Preparation

You will need a sheet of 8½ x 11" paper and scissors for this story. Fold the sheet of paper in half, lengthwise, as shown in the illustration.

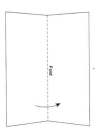

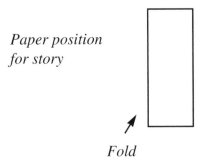

Paper position for story

Fold

Be sure to hold the fold *vertically* and cut from the right side. Make your cuts exactly as shown in the illustrations; otherwise the finished product will not work.

Tell the following story while making the cuts as shown in the illustrations.

John had not been feeling like himself lately. In fact, he was feeling like half of himself. John was seeing one half of everything! **THIS IS ONE HALF OF JOHN'S HOUSE.** *(Hold up cut-out piece.)*

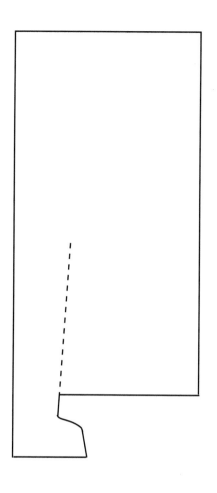

John locked his door and walked down one half of a **VERY NARROW SIDEWALK.** As he looked down at his feet, it seemed he only had one half of his legs. Instead of two, there was only one!

John quickly blinked his eyes to be sure he was only seeing things. When he opened his eyes, he saw something even stranger— **A BIRD WITH ONLY ONE WING!** *(Hold up cut-out piece.)*

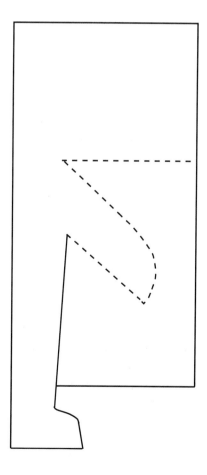

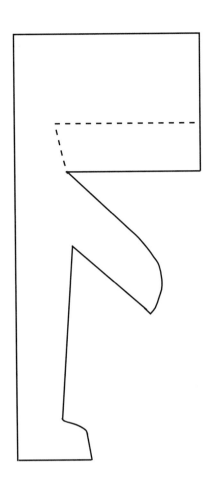

John **WALKED ON,** trying to figure out what his problem was.

Walking around what looked like **ONE HALF OF A CIRCULAR POND,** John looked into the water and saw his reflection. He now knew what his problem was and what to do about it.

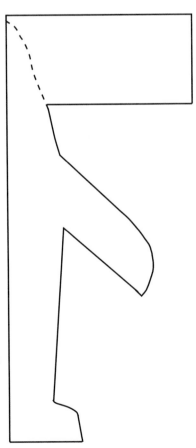

John made a quick trip to see his twin brother Joe. After spending some time together and having a lot of fun, John was soon feeling whole again. It took seeing his other half to feel more like himself. How do you think John made the trip to see Joe? *(Unfold the paper.)*

The Thing with Three Humps

Preparation

You will need a sheet of 8½ x 11" paper and scissors for this story. Fold the sheet of paper in half, lengthwise, as shown in the illustration.

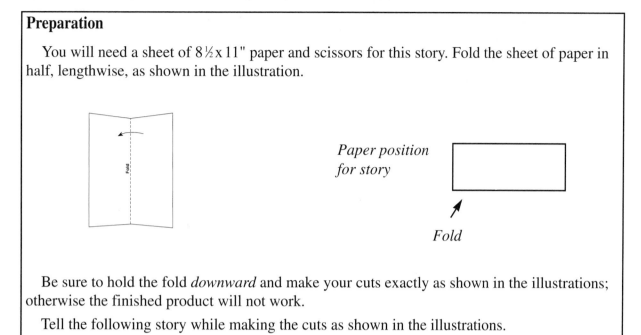

*Paper position
for story*

Fold

Be sure to hold the fold *downward* and make your cuts exactly as shown in the illustrations; otherwise the finished product will not work.

Tell the following story while making the cuts as shown in the illustrations.

Frank was out of school for the summer. At first it was fun, but he soon ran out of things to do. He also ran out of money.

"You need a job," said his mother. "Go down to the park and see if you can find some work."

Frank **WALKED UP ONE SIDE OF PARK HILL AND DOWN THE OTHER.** He couldn't believe what he saw.

There were more people at the park than Frank had ever seen before. They were all standing around the park's old pond. The hot sun reflected off the water and made everyone squint. Frank had to find out what everyone was watching. He pushed through the crowd. He couldn't get through. He had to stand behind **TWO BALD MEN.** This is what he saw:

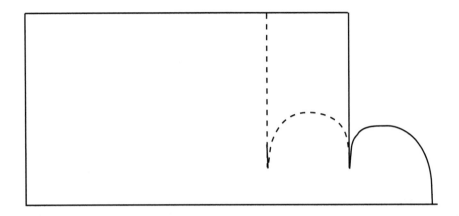

Frank finally found someone his own size. He asked the young girl what was going on. She told him that Mrs. Cooler, who lived across the street, had called the park ranger. Mrs. Cooler told the park ranger she had seen something in the pond.

"Some kind of rare fish?" asked Frank.

"No, not at all," answered the girl. "She said it was a sea monster. A big green thing with shiny scales and a long, thin neck."

"And humps?" asked Frank.

"Yes," said the girl. **"THREE OF THEM."**

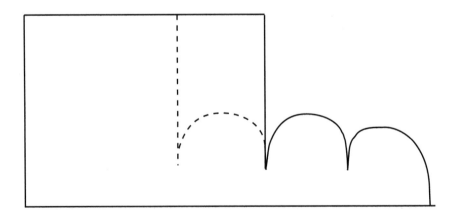

Just then, Frank had an idea. The people were here to see the monster. They would probably have to stand out in the bright sun for a long time to catch a glimpse of the beast. Frank knew he had found his summer job. He quickly ran home to get his parents' **ICE CHEST.** He brought this back to the park.

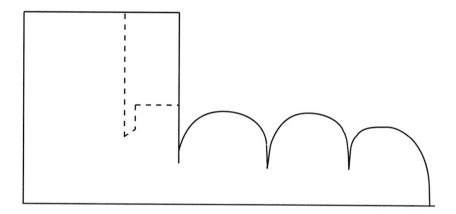

As soon as Frank came back over the hill he smiled. There were even more people watching the water than before! He quickly found a **LONG SPACE ON THE SIDEWALK** and opened for business.

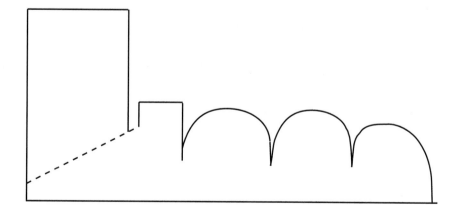

No one ever did see Mrs. Cooler's monster, but Frank didn't mind. He made enough money to pay for a trip to Ride World. He did this by selling his special creation: The Mrs. Cooler Three Hump Monster Cone. *(Unfold the paper.)*

Will It Ever Snow?

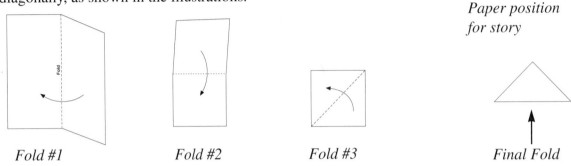
   "Will it ever snow?" asked Tracy as she looked longingly at her new sled.

   "Oh, I'm sure you won't have to wait much longer, honey," said her mother.

   "Gosh, I can hardly wait to try out the new sled Grandma and Grandpa gave me for my birthday."

   "Well, for what it's worth, yesterday's newspaper said we can expect a snowfall sometime today."

   "I sure hope so," said Tracy. Then, walking to the closet she added, "I think I will go over to Amy and Seth's house."

   "Okay, but be sure to bundle up. It's terribly cold out."

(Cut on dotted lines in each of the illustrations. Fold must be held downward.)

   Tracy first put on her **HEAVY WINTER COAT.**

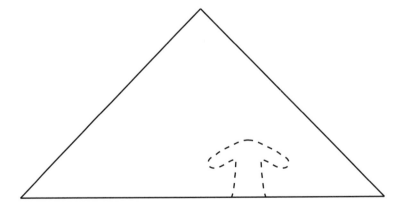

Then she sat down on the floor and tugged on first **ONE BOOT** . . .

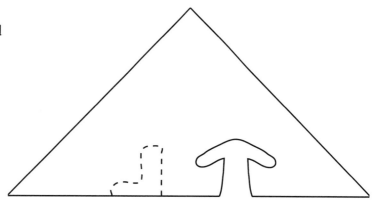

. . . and then **THE OTHER ONE.**

"I'm going now," said Tracy, starting for the back door.

"Wait just a minute, young lady," said her mother. "You forgot your hat and earmuffs. Why, you'll freeze your ears off!"

Tracy giggled and said, "But I'm only going across the street."

"But what if Amy and Seth want to play outside?"

"Why on Earth would they want to without any snow?"

"Well, you just never can tell."

"Okay, I'll put them on," said Tracy. "But I don't know where they are."

"On the top shelf in the closet," responded her mother.

Tracy simply did not know how her mother always seemed to know where everything was!

"Yes . . . here they are," she said as she put **THE EARMUFFS** over her ears.

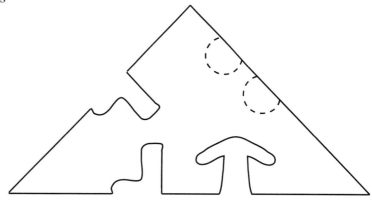

"And your hat is hanging on the side hook, in back of your father's jacket."

Tracy removed the jacket to find her hat right where her mother said it would be. She shook her head as she placed **THE HAT** on her head and said goodbye.

As soon as Tracy began to cross the street, she felt something on her nose. It was cold and wet. *(Begin unfolding the paper.)*

She looked up and saw large beautiful snowflakes floating down from the sky.

"Hooray!" she said out loud. "Soon we can go sledding!"

My Uncle, the Artist

Preparation

You will need a sheet of 8½ x 11" paper and scissors for this story. Fold the sheet of paper in half, widthwise, as shown in the illustration.

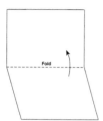

 Paper position for story

Fold

Be sure to hold the fold *downward* and make your cuts exactly as shown in the illustrations; otherwise the finished product will not work.

Tell the following story while making the cuts as shown in the illustrations.

"Wow, this sure is some place," exclaimed Marty.

"I knew you'd like it," said her friend Sara.

"What did you call it?"

"It's my uncle's studio."

"Gosh, a real artist's studio. It even smells special."

Sara laughed, "Oh, that's the paints and other things he uses in his art."

"And everywhere you look is art!" exclaimed Marty.

"Look up," said Sara.

"Oh gosh . . . a window in the ceiling!"

"Yes, it is called a **SKYLIGHT.**"

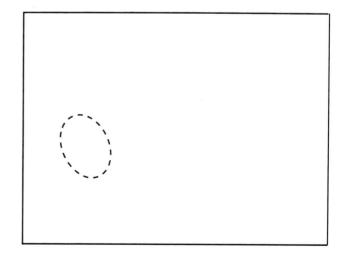

"My uncle says that all artists need a lot of *natural* light in order to paint."

"Is this where he paints?" asked Marty, pointing to an easel.

"Yes, and there is one of his **PAINTBRUSHES.**"

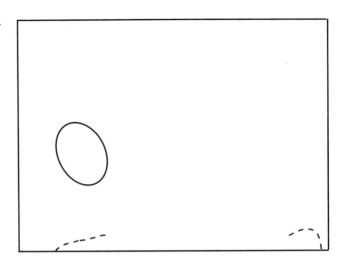

"What's that?" asked Marty, pointing to something next to the brush.

"Oh, that's my uncle's **PAINT PALETTE.**"

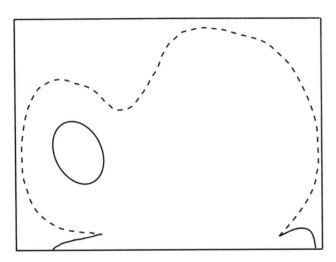

"That is where he puts the paints he uses while working," explained Sara. "Here, I'll show you."

"Are you sure you should touch it?"

"Of course. My uncle lets me paint whenever I want to."

"Boy, you sure are lucky."

"Yes, I know," said Sara. "See, you squeeze **A LITTLE RED PAINT HERE** . . .

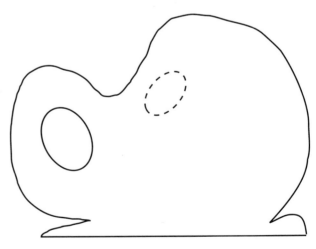

. . . and **BLUE PAINT** here. . .

. . . and **YELLOW PAINT** here."

"Oops!" said Sara as she **DRIPPED SOME OF THE PAINT.**

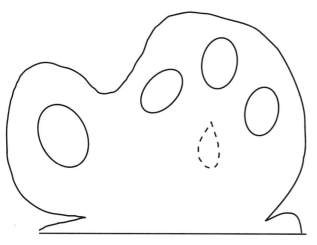

25

"Do you think I could paint here sometime?" asked Marty.

"Sure. My uncle loves to have company while he's painting."

"Hi, girls!"

"Oh, hi, Uncle Evan. This is my friend, Tracy."

"Well, what do you think, Tracy?"

"I love your studio Mr. . . ."

"Just call me Evan. Well, I see you have my palette ready to use, so why don't I use it to paint a special picture for Tracy."

The girls stood mesmerized as Evan painted a beautiful picture. When he finished he said, "You may have this Tracy, after it dries."

Tracy was so excited she could hardly wait to get home to tell her parents what Evan had painted for her.

Do you think you can guess what it was? *(Unfold the paper for the children to see.)*

Jacob's Gift

Preparation

You will need a sheet of 8½ x 11" paper and scissors for this story. Fold the sheet of paper in half, widthwise, as shown in the illustration.

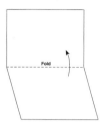

Paper position for story

Fold

Be sure to hold the fold *downward* and make your cuts exactly as shown in the illustrations; otherwise the finished product will not work.

Tell the following story while making the cuts as shown in the illustrations.

The town of Monroe was having a celebration—a celebration of 100 years, to be exact. It had been 100 years since Monroe had become a town.

Monroe sat at the **TOP OF A LONG SLOPING HILL.** It was a small, friendly town—friendly, that is, except for Jacob Brown.

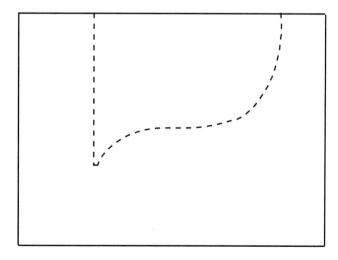

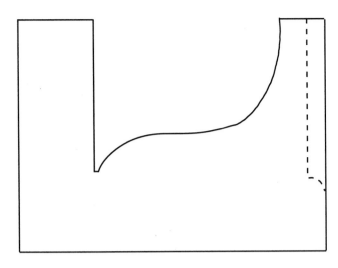

Jacob lived on a **SMALLER HILL BEHIND MONROE.** He was not a particularly friendly individual.

In fact, Jacob had been meaner than ever lately. He used to stare at people who walked by his place. Now he wouldn't even look out of his tiny workshop.

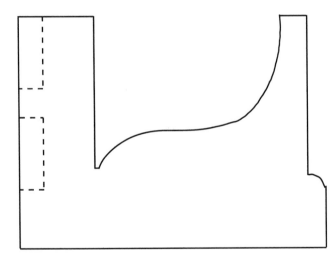

It wasn't too long before people started walking quite a bit **OUT OF THEIR WAY** to stay away from Jacob's place.

With the town's celebration upon them, the townsfolk forgot all about Jacob. They kept busy planning for the 100th birthday of Monroe. Jacob, however, wasn't to be forgotten so easily. He pulled into town right during the middle of the celebration. He was hauling a big crate. With the help of some townsfolk he sat it **RIGHT IN THE MIDDLE OF THE MONROE TOWN SQUARE.**

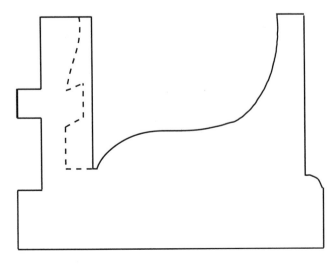

The mayor of Monroe opened the crate. The whole town was shocked. Jacob has been so grumpy lately because he was working on a special gift for the town. Jacob even seemed to smile as the townsfolk thanked him for their treasure. This was Jacob's gift. *(Unfold the paper.)*

Uncle Merlin's Magic

Preparation

You will need a sheet of 8½ x 11" paper and scissors for this story. Fold the sheet of paper in half, widthwise, as shown in the illustration.

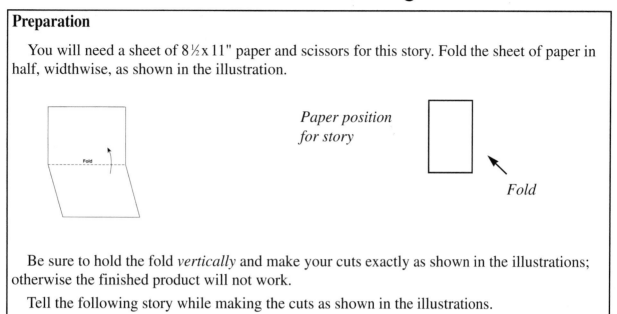

Paper position for story

Fold

Be sure to hold the fold *vertically* and make your cuts exactly as shown in the illustrations; otherwise the finished product will not work.

Tell the following story while making the cuts as shown in the illustrations.

David and Sharie went to visit their Uncle Merlin one afternoon. Merlin was not your normal uncle. He was quite different from any other of Sharie and David's relatives. Take his house, for example. It sat **AT THE BASE OF A CLIFF,** tucked in darkness and mystery.

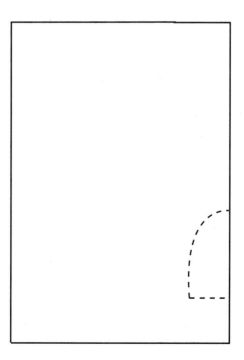

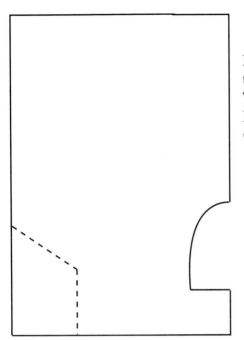

When David and Sharie arrived, they knocked on Merlin's door. No one answered. Sharie grinned at David as they both nodded. Of course, he would be in his workshop. They quickly ran to the other side of the hill. Uncle Merlin's workshop **SAT HERE UNDER A ROCKY CLIFF.**

David and Sharie knew Uncle Merlin would not be able to hear them knock on the door. They simply pushed open the door and went inside. Uncle Merlin's house was as unusual as Uncle Merlin. They took a burning candle and began **DOWN THE TWISTED AND TURNING PATH TO UNCLE MERLIN'S WORKSHOP.**

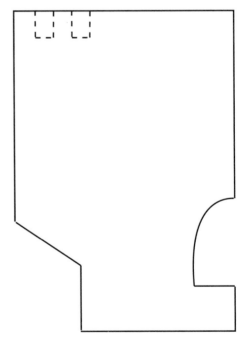

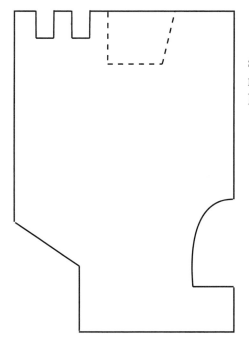

As soon as they entered the workshop, David and Sharie saw something they had never seen before. Right in the middle of the workshop floor was **A TRAP DOOR**—a large, *opened* trap door.

The children called out for their uncle.

"Down here, dears," came the reply. "Come down, but mind your step."

The children **CAREFULLY MADE THEIR WAY DOWN INTO THE DARKNESS.**

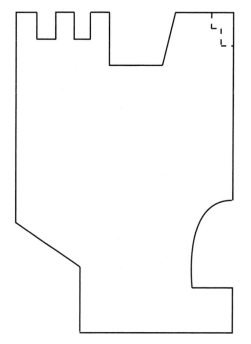

Once inside the cavern, the children rubbed their eyes in disbelief.

"Do you like it?" asked Uncle Merlin. "It's my latest project."

The children could only nod as they stood speechless in front of Uncle Merlin's masterpiece. It was a glittering, life-size . . . *(Unfold the paper.)*

Samuel Seagull

Preparation

You will need a sheet of 8½ x 11" paper and scissors for this story. Fold the sheet of paper in half, lengthwise, as shown in the illustration.

Paper position for story

Fold

Fold

Be sure to hold the fold *vertically* and make your cuts exactly as shown in the illustrations; otherwise the finished product will not work.

Tell the following story while making the cuts as shown in the illustrations.

Samuel Seagull was a very worldly bird. He had flown over many countries, fished in many oceans, and visited many islands. Samuel thought that because he had been so very many places, he should be so very smart. Usually Samuel did know what was going on. Occasionally, however, he would see something he knew nothing about. Today was one of those days.

Samuel had almost flown right into whatever it was! Looking back over his shoulder, Samuel became very, very scared at what he saw. It was definitely a monster. As fast as he could, **HE FLEW BACK TO HIS FRIENDS ON THE SEA COAST.**

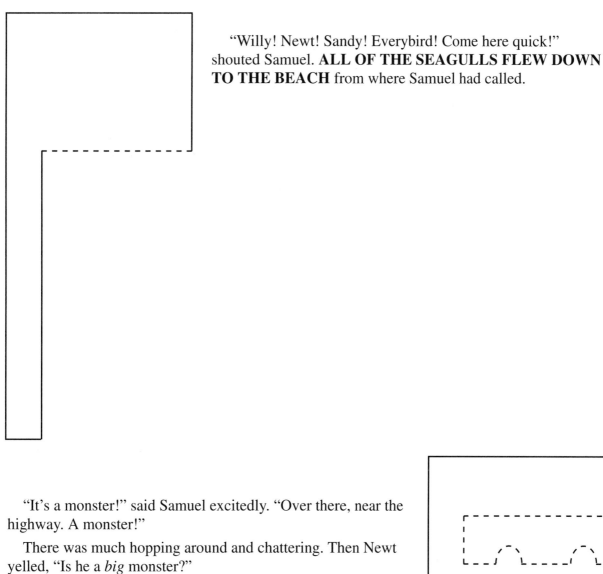

"Willy! Newt! Sandy! Everybird! Come here quick!" shouted Samuel. **ALL OF THE SEAGULLS FLEW DOWN TO THE BEACH** from where Samuel had called.

"It's a monster!" said Samuel excitedly. "Over there, near the highway. A monster!"

There was much hopping around and chattering. Then Newt yelled, "Is he a *big* monster?"

"Oh yes," said Samuel, "and **HE HAS A HUGE MOUTH WITH TWO LARGE TEETH.**"

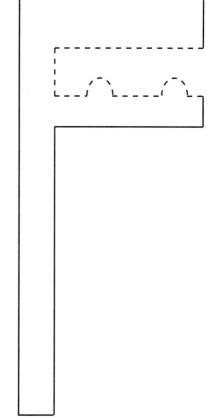

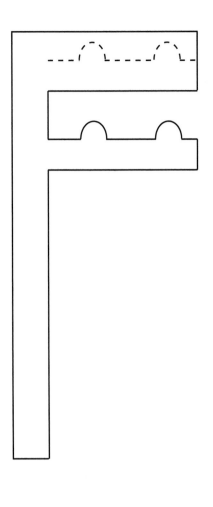

All of the seagulls were silent. Willy then asked quietly, "Does it eat seagulls?"

"I don't know," answered Samuel.

"Can it fly?" asked Sandy.

"Maybe," said Samuel. "I didn't see it move, but I did see that **IT HAD TWO EVIL LOOKING EYES** that kept glaring at me."

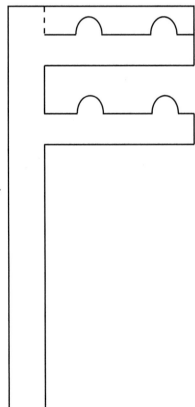

All of the birds looked at Samuel as Newt asked, "What should we do?"

Samuel thought for a long time and then said, "I think we should find another beach on which to live and fish." They all quickly agreed and **FLEW AWAY** in the opposite direction of the monster.

Do you think you know what the monster really was?
(*Unfold the paper.*)

The Magic Forest

Preparation

You will need a sheet of 8½ x 14" paper and scissors for this story. Fold the sheet of paper in half, widthwise. Now fold it two more times in the same direction, forming a rectangle 8½ x 1¾", as shown in the illustrations.

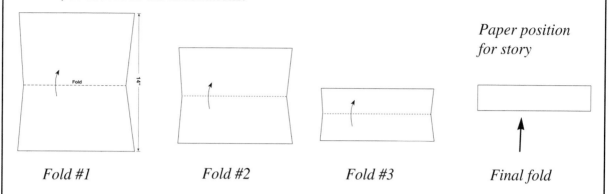

Fold #1 *Fold #2* *Fold #3* *Final fold*

Paper position for story

Be sure to hold the final fold *downward* and make your cuts exactly as shown in the illustrations; otherwise the finished product will not work.

Tell the following story while making the cuts as shown in the illustrations.

It was such a strange dream that Little Cloud could think of nothing else. How strange for a Navajo to dream of something he had never seen before! Imagine a tree so large you could climb almost up to the sky—or at least it seemed so in his dream. Little Cloud had never seen a real tree before, so why would he have dreamed of not one, but *many*. Indeed, it had been a forest—a "magic" forest—in his dream.

Little Cloud walked with his friend, Lone Wolf, out to the mesa. Sitting on the edge, the two could look down into the deep canyon. It was here that Little Cloud told his friend of his strange dream.

"It's on the far side of this canyon," said Little Cloud. "The magic forest is there . . . I just know it. The great spirit came to me in my dream and told me to find the magic forest. Then he pointed across the canyon in that direction."

Lone Wolf said nothing but simply nodded his head and stared out into the canyon. Without having to say it, the two friends knew what they had to do.

Early the next morning, Little Cloud and Lone Wolf stood at the edge of the mesa. It would be hot crossing the floor of the canyon, so they wanted to get an early start.

DOWN THE CANYON WALL THEY DESCENDED until they reached the canyon floor.

35

They looked back up the mesa from which they began. They each had the same thought: It would be a lot slower going back up than it was coming down.

Both boys turned away from the wall and began their long journey **ACROSS THE DESERT.**

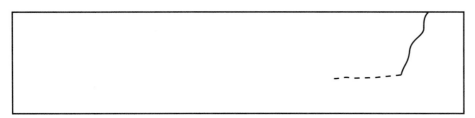

After what seemed like forever, they came to **A SMALL MESA** which they went around.

Once on the other side, they stopped to have a drink.

"How much farther?" asked Lone Wolf.

"I don't know," answered Little Cloud. "The Great Spirit only pointed **IN THAT DIRECTION.**"

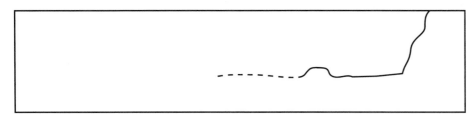

So the two boys headed off once again into **THE BLAZING SUN** . . .

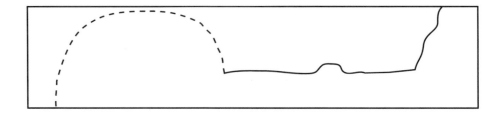

. . . with hopes of discovering the Magic Forest. *(Begin unfolding paper.)*

Do you think Little Cloud and Lone Wolf ever discovered the Magic Forest?

Gussy G.

Preparation

You will need a sheet of 8½ x 11" paper and scissors for this story. Fold the sheet of paper in half, lengthwise, as shown in the illustration.

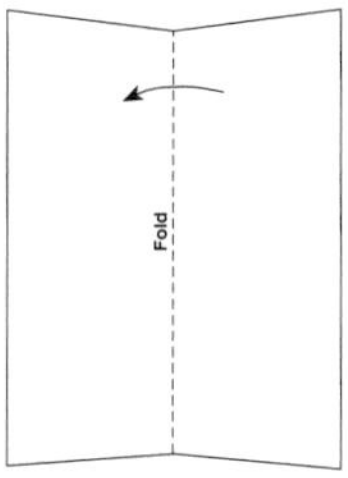

Fold

Paper position for story

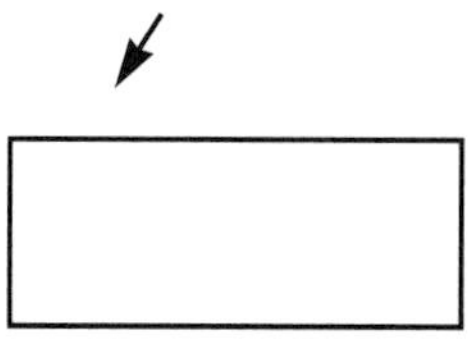

Be sure to hold the fold *upward* and make your cuts exactly as shown in the illustrations; otherwise the finished product will not work.

Tell the following story while making the cuts as shown in the illustrations.

Now Gussy G. was a sweet old girl,

A good old girl from the south.

Gussy G. could be a mean old girl,

for **THESE WERE THE THINGS IN HER MOUTH.**

(Point to sharp point.)

Now Gussy G. wasn't awful mean,

Like a snake hanging down from a tree.

No, she was only nasty if you bothered her,

Kind of **LIKE A BIG OLD STINGING BEE.**

(Point to sharp point.)

Gussy G. didn't bother a soul,

As long as a soul didn't pass.

You see, Gussy G. lived on a **QUIET ISLAND**

Covered in lush green grass.

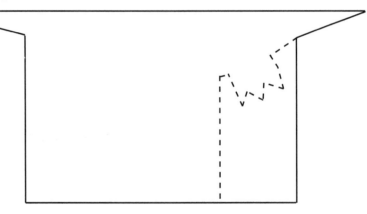

One fine day not so long ago,

Petunia Snuff went out,

She passed by Gussy G.'s place,

And **STAYED FAR AWAY,** no doubt.

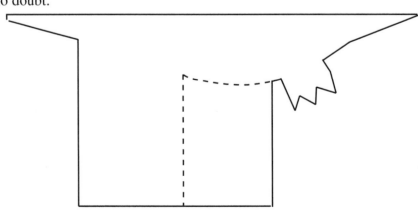

Petunia Snuff was safe she thought,
She'd let old Gussy be.
But one old **GREEN ISLAND** can look like another,
I guess Petunia didn't see.

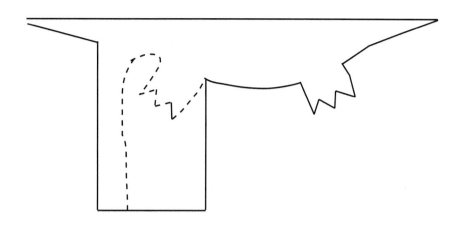

But Gussy saw, she did I swear,
She saw Petunia snackin',
She **WENT AROUND PETUNIA'S FEET,**
And got her lips to smackin'.

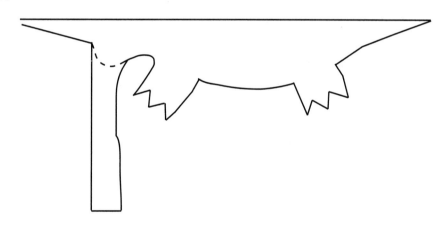

Old Gussy surprised Miss Snuff,
She surprised her and she ate her.
But you all can't blame old Gussy G.,
She's just an alligator! *(Unfold the paper.)*

Where Is Pepito?

Preparation

You will need a sheet of 8 x 8" paper and scissors for this story. Fold the sheet of paper in half and then fold it again to form a 4 x 4" square, as shown in the illustrations.

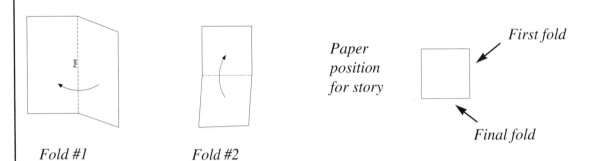

Fold #1   *Fold #2*   *Paper position for story*   *First fold*   *Final fold*

Be sure to hold the final fold *downward* and make your cuts exactly as shown in the illustrations; otherwise the finished product will not work.

Tell the following story while making the cuts as shown in the illustrations.

Carlitos hurried into the kitchen where his mother was cooking.

"Yum," said Carlitos. "I smell something good."

"Yes," laughed his mother. "And you know very well what it is *and* that you must wait until dinner."

Carlitos' mother was cooking his favorite meal . . . tamales. She used **A LARGE KETTLE** of boiling water.

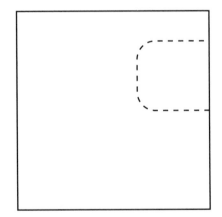

"Why don't you go down to the marketplace and look for Papa. He should be coming home soon and *then* we will have our tamales."

"All right, Mama," said Carlitos, and hurried out the door.

"Come on, Pepito," he called to his little dog.

Pepito was chewing on **A LARGE, HALF-EATEN BONE** . . .

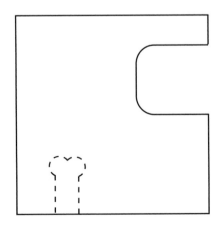

. . . but when he heard Carlitos, he dropped the bone and came running.

The two hurried down the narrow street toward the marketplace. As soon as they arrived, Carlitos saw a man in a large **STRAW HAT** . . .

. . . who was selling sweet dough churros.

"Hi, Leandro," said Carlitos.

"Hi, Carlitos, my little friend. How would you like one of my sweet churros?"

"Oh yes, Leandro."

Leandro smiled and handed Carlitos one of his fresh churros.

"Thank you, Leandro."

"You are welcome, my friend."

Carlitos took a huge bite of his churros as he made his way through the crowd. Across the street he could see the lady selling her colorful **BALLOONS.**

"Come on, Pepito, we'd better hurry to Papa's store."

Carlitos looked all around him, but he did not see his little dog.

"Pepito," he called, but the noise in the marketplace was so loud he knew his little dog would never hear him.

"Now, where could he have gone?" Carlitos thought to himself. He hurried **DOWN THE STREET** . . .

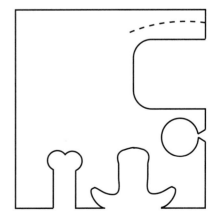

41

. . . to **THE BAKERY AND WENT AROUND THE BUILDING** calling for Pepito. But his dog was not there.

"Oh, I know," Carlitos thought, and hurried **ACROSS THE STREET** . . .

. . . to the butcher shop. He went **DOWN THE ALLEY AND AROUND THE SHOP** calling for Pepito. But Pepito was not there.

Carlitos decided to go to his papa's fruit store since Pepito often went there. He **WALKED UP THE STREET** toward the plaza.

He hurried into the fruit store.

"Papa, Papa, Pepito is missing!" called Carlitos.

"Hi, Carlitos," said his father. "Maybe he is out in back. Why don't you look around the store while I close up for the day."

So Carlitos **LOOKED ALL AROUND THE STORE.**

"Papa, I still haven't found Pepito," said Carlitos as he hurried back into the store.

His father was putting away the last of the fruits. "Well, why don't we have a look around the plaza before heading home."

Carlitos and his father **WALKED DOWN TO THE PLAZA.** *(Begin unfolding the paper.)*

"There he is," said Carlitos, laughing.

"Where?" asked his father.

"Sitting under that large pinata!"

The Hiking Incident

Preparation

You will need a sheet of 8 ½ x 11" paper and scissors for this story. Fold the sheet of paper in half, lengthwise, as shown in the illustration.

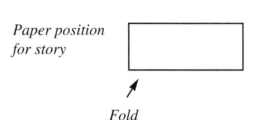

Paper position for story

Fold

Be sure to hold the fold *downward* and make your cuts exactly as shown in the illustrations; otherwise the finished product will not work.

Tell the following story while making the cuts as shown in the illustrations.

"Whew, it sure is hot," complained Mike.

"Aw, is it too hot for 'ittle Mikey?" teased his best friend Greg.

"No, but I bet this is too hot for 'ittle Greggie!" returned Mike as he walloped Greg on the back with his backpack.

"Hey!" yelled Greg as he returned a wallop to Mike. Both boys fell down in the grass wrestling and laughing.

"I need a drink," said Greg.

"Me too," agreed Mike as he tugged at the canteen in his backpack. Both boys took long drinks from their canteens.

"Not much farther," said Mike, looking up the trail.

It was Saturday and the two friends had decided to spend the day hiking up Twin Peaks.

The townsfolk had called the two large hills Twin Peaks for as long as anyone could remember. They were located about a mile outside of town and were not really "twin" peaks at all. Actually one was considerably smaller. It was **THIS SMALLER HILL** that the boys had hiked up last summer.

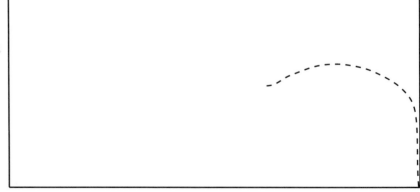

But today they were almost to **THE TOP OF THE LARGER PEAK.**

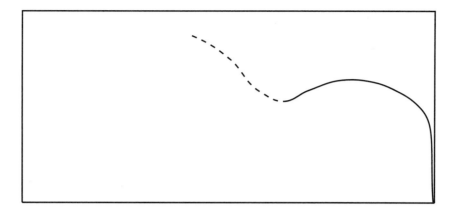

"We had better not waste any more time. This climb is taking longer than we thought it would," said Greg.

"Yeah, you're right," agreed Mike. So the boys hurried to **THE TOP OF THE PEAK.**

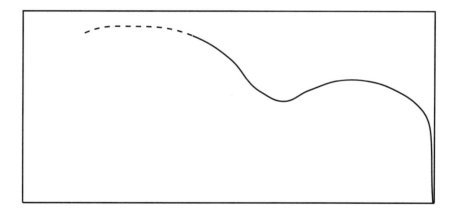

By the time they arrived at the top, **THE SUN WAS BEGINNING TO GO DOWN.**

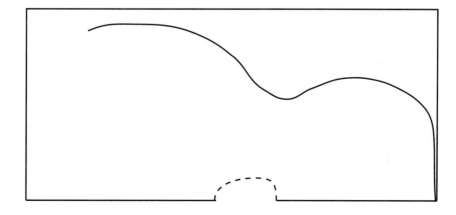

"We made it," said Greg triumphantly.

"We sure did, but it's a good thing we brought our flashlights," said Mike.

"Yeah . . . we'll probably need them before we get back to town," agreed Greg.

So the boys immediately began their hike **DOWN THE OTHER SIDE OF THE HILL.**

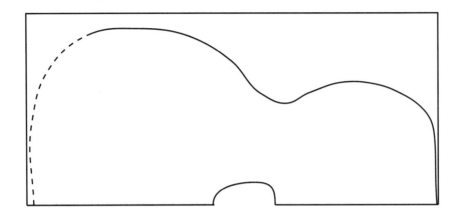

Because it was getting dark and they were in a hurry, the boys didn't see **THE OLD WELL** until it was too late.

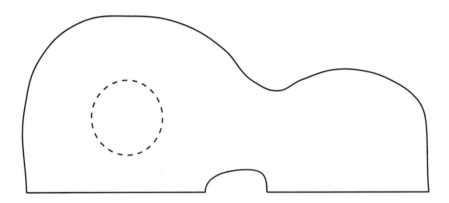

"Yeow!" they both yelled as they tumbled down the shallow well.

"Oooff!" groaned Greg as Mike bumped into him at the bottom of the well.

"Boy, this is just great," complained Mike as he turned on his flashlight.

Both boys were quiet as they looked around the old well.

"It shouldn't be very hard to climb out of this old well," said Greg.

"No, it isn't very deep, thank goodness."

"Look over there," said Greg, shining his flashlight at **AN OPENING IN THE WALL.**

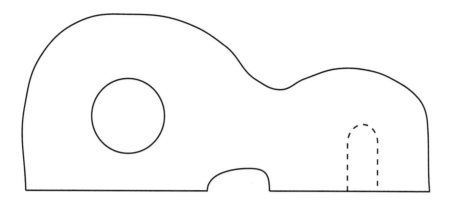

"Gosh," said Mike quietly. "What do you think is in there?"

"Let's take a look," said Greg.

As the two boys entered the opening, they both yelled and scrambled up and out of the well as fast as they could!

Now what do you suppose they saw that scared them so? *(Unfold the paper.)*

The Muddywater Mystery

Preparation

You will need a sheet of 8½ x 11" paper and scissors for this story. Fold the sheet of paper in half, lengthwise, as shown in the illustration.

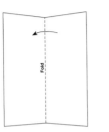

Starting paper position for story

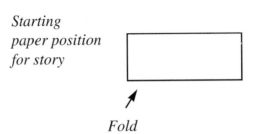

Fold

Be sure to hold the fold as instructed in the illustrations and make your cuts exactly as shown; otherwise the finished product will not work.

Tell the following story while making the cuts as shown in the illustrations.

Mia Python, famous private investigator, was called to the location of the Muddywater Annual Carnival. Velma Guesser, the carnival's fortuneteller, was missing. Foul play was suspected, so the owner had called Mia at home. Mia had been napping and she **ARCHED HER SCALY BACK** as they talked on the phone.

Quickly she **SLITHERED UP THE HILL** to the carnival.

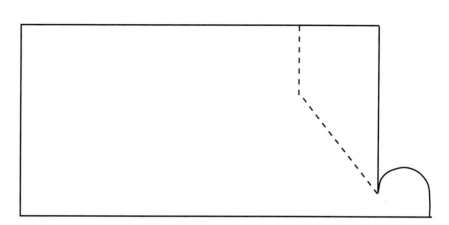

(Turn paper so fold is now upward.)

Fold

Once at the carnival, Mia **SLITHERED INTO VELMA'S TENT** to search for clues.

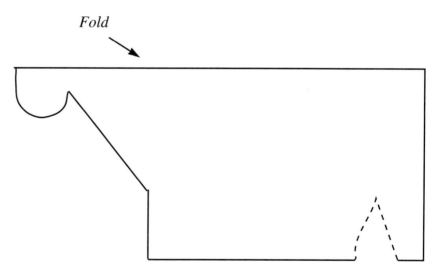

As Mia **WRAPPED HERSELF AROUND VELMA'S TABLE,** she noticed some paper under Velma's chair.

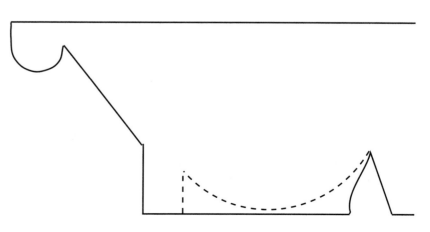

Mia knew this might be a clue, so she used her **LONG TONGUE** to pull the paper from beneath the chair.

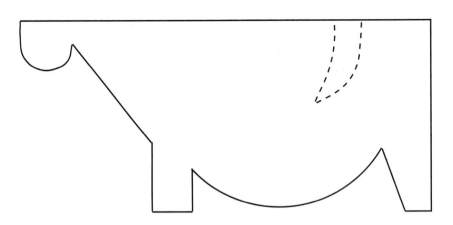

Mia felt the earth tremble and quickly **CURLED UP INTO A SMALL CIRCLE.** *(Hold up cut-out circle.)* Someone walked into Velma's tent.

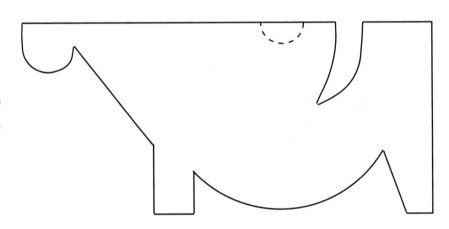

Mia looked at the stranger's feet from under the table. The stranger had **TWO LONG, ROUND FEET.** *(Hold up round pieces.)*

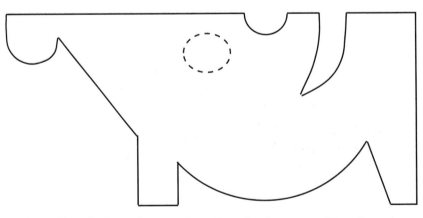

Mia then knew that Velma wasn't really missing, she was just disguised as one of her favorite carnival performers. *(Unfold the paper.)*

The Spoiled Princess

Preparation

You will need a sheet of 8½ x 11" paper and scissors for this story. Fold the sheet of paper in half, widthwise, as shown in the illustration.

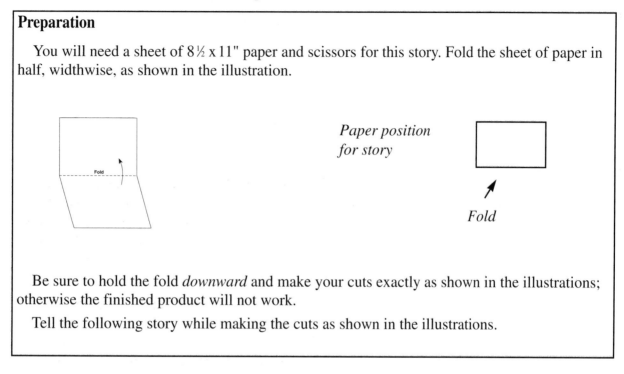

Paper position for story

Fold

Be sure to hold the fold *downward* and make your cuts exactly as shown in the illustrations; otherwise the finished product will not work.

Tell the following story while making the cuts as shown in the illustrations.

There once lived a Princess in a faraway land. Her mother and father, the King and Queen, gave her anything she wanted. Whenever she would wish for something, she simply would **GO TO THE THRONE ROOM.**

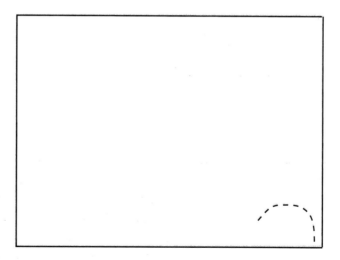

Once there, she would tell her mother and father what she wanted. If they so much as even hesitated in complying with the Princess's wishes, she would fly into a rage and stomp around the throne room yelling at everyone in sight. She was, indeed, a very spoiled little Princess.

51

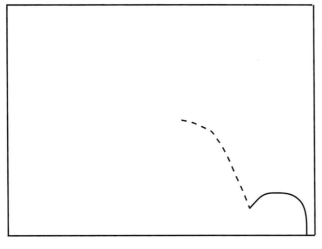

One day, without telling anyone, she left the castle and **WENT TO THE NEARBY VILLAGE.**

Now the Princess had been told many, many times never to go into the village alone, but, you'll recall, she was not a very nice Princess. So she giggled to herself as she slipped out of the castle without anyone seeing her.

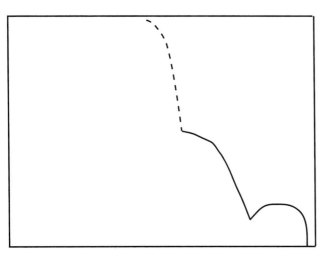

The villagers had never seen the Princess outside the castle without her nanny and several soldiers, so you can imagine their surprise. **SHE WALKED RIGHT INTO THE BAKER'S SHOP** . . .

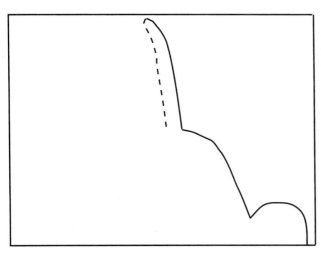

. . . pushed in front of the other customers, and demanded a sweet muffin. Since she was the Princess, the baker's wife immediately handed her the largest and sweetest muffin in the shop. Without so much as a "Thank you, ma'am," she shoved the muffin in her mouth and **STRODE OUT OF THE SHOP.**

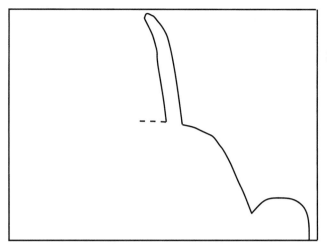

With a trail of muffin crumbs following her, she **MADE HER WAY TO THE NEXT SHOP.**

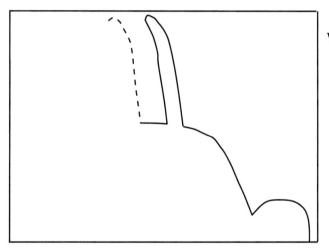

She pushed two ladies out of her way and **WALKED INTO THE PRODUCE SHOP.**

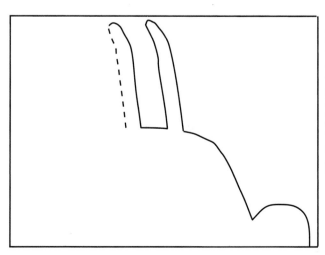

There were vegetables and fruits stacked in large bins and crates. The Princess didn't wait to be asked, she just loudly demanded the largest and juiciest apple in the shop. Since she was the Princess, the owner immediately handed her the largest and juiciest apple he had. Without so much as a "Thank you, sir," she shoved the apple in her mouth and **STRODE OUT OF THE SHOP.**

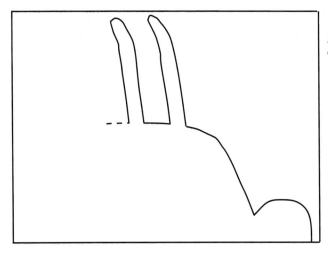

Followed by a trail of apple skins, seeds, and core bits the Princess **MADE HER WAY TO THE NEXT SHOP.**

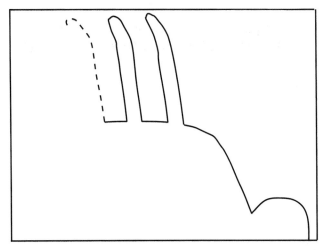

She didn't hesitate for a second, but **PUSHED HER WAY INTO THE CANDY SHOP.**

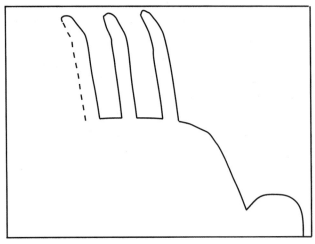

There were licorice sticks, chocolate drops, and every other kind of candy you can imagine in the shop's cases. She didn't wait to be asked, she just yelled for the largest sack of jellybeans in the shop. Since she was the Princess, the lady behind the counter immediately handed her the largest sack filled with the sweetest jellybeans in the shop. Without so much as a "Thank you, ma'am," she shoved a handful of jellybeans in her mouth and **STRODE OUT OF THE SHOP.**

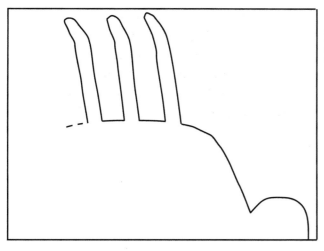

With a trail of jellybeans following her, the Princess **MADE HER WAY TO THE NEXT SHOP.**

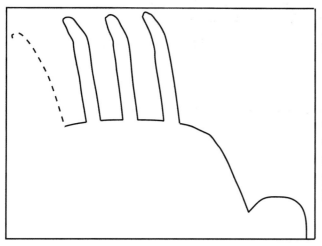

There were two boys in her way, so she just pushed them aside and **WALKED INTO THE TOY SHOP.**

There were puppets, balls, dolls, jumpropes, and every other kind of toy imaginable on the shelves in the shop. The Princess didn't wait to be asked, she just demanded that the owner put his very best toy in a sack for her to take back to the castle.

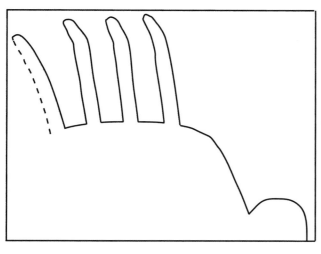

Now, the owner wanted to please the Princess, but he didn't know which of his toys to give her. A small boy who had been following her since she entered the village and seen how rude she had been, slipped over to the owner, and whispered in his ear. The owner smiled as he reached down behind the counter and placed something in a small sack. Without so much as a "Thank you, sir," the Princess grabbed the sack and **STRODE OUT OF THE SHOP.**

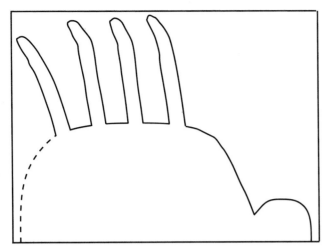

Once out of the toy shop, the princess opened the sack and reached in to pull out her toy. The villagers were shocked when the Princess let out a loud shriek and **RAN ALL THE WAY BACK TO THE CASTLE** without stopping once.

At dinnertime, the King and Queen were surprised to find their little Princess quiet and very polite. She didn't yell when she wanted something, nor did she stomp around the dining room when she found out they were not having her favorite dessert, chocolate chip ice cream.

The King looked at the Queen and said, "Something really must have scared her for her to be so good!" *(Begin to unfold the paper.)*

Now, what do you think was in that little sack that scared the Princess so much?